Coloring Lifestyles

Yah's Majesty

A Gray Scale Journey

Before the mountains were born or you brought forth the wide world, from everlasting to everlasting, you are God.

Psalms 90:2

Donna S. Hale

ColoringLifestyles.com

Are you anxious for your book to arrive in the mailbox? No worries!
There is immediate gratification for your worried little self---so calm
down! Visit ColoringLifestyles.com for information on how you can
get 4 gorgeous, printable coloring sheets FREE!
Start coloring today and before you know it, your coloring book
will have arrived in the mail! Happy coloring and CONGRATULATIONS!

Dedicated to Donald
The love of my life

Thank you for believing in me!

Then the angel showed me the river of the water of life, bright as crystal, flowing from the throne of God and the Lamb.
Revelation 22:1

He made the storm be still, and the waves of the sea was hushed.

Psalms 107:29

....He leadeth me beside still waters

Psalms 23:2

From the rising of the sun unto the going down of the same,
the Lord's name is to be praised.

Psalms 113:3

Before the mountains were born or you brought forth the wide world, from everlasting to everlasting, you are God.

Psalms 90:2

The righteous flourish like the palm tree
and grow like a cedar in Lebanon.
Psalms 92:12

I am the Lord your God, who stirs up the seas so that its waves roar. Isaiah 51:15

Like cold water to a thirsty soul, so is good news from a far country.

Proverbs 25:25

But they that wait upon the Lord shall renew their strength; they shall mount up with wings as eagles.....

Isaiah 40:31

Sing to the Lord a new song; sing to the Lord all the earth.

Psalms 96:1

Hear, O Israel, The Lord our God, the Lord is One.
Deuteronomy 6:4

He reached down from on high and took hold of me;

he drew me out of deep water.

2 Samuel 22:17

For I will satisfy the weary soul, and every languishing soul will I replenish.

Jeremiah 31:25

Every tithe of the land, whether of the seed of the land, or the fruit of the tree's is the Lord's.

Leviticus 27:30

Everyone then who hears these words of mine and does them will be like a wise man who built his house on a rock.

Matthew 7:24

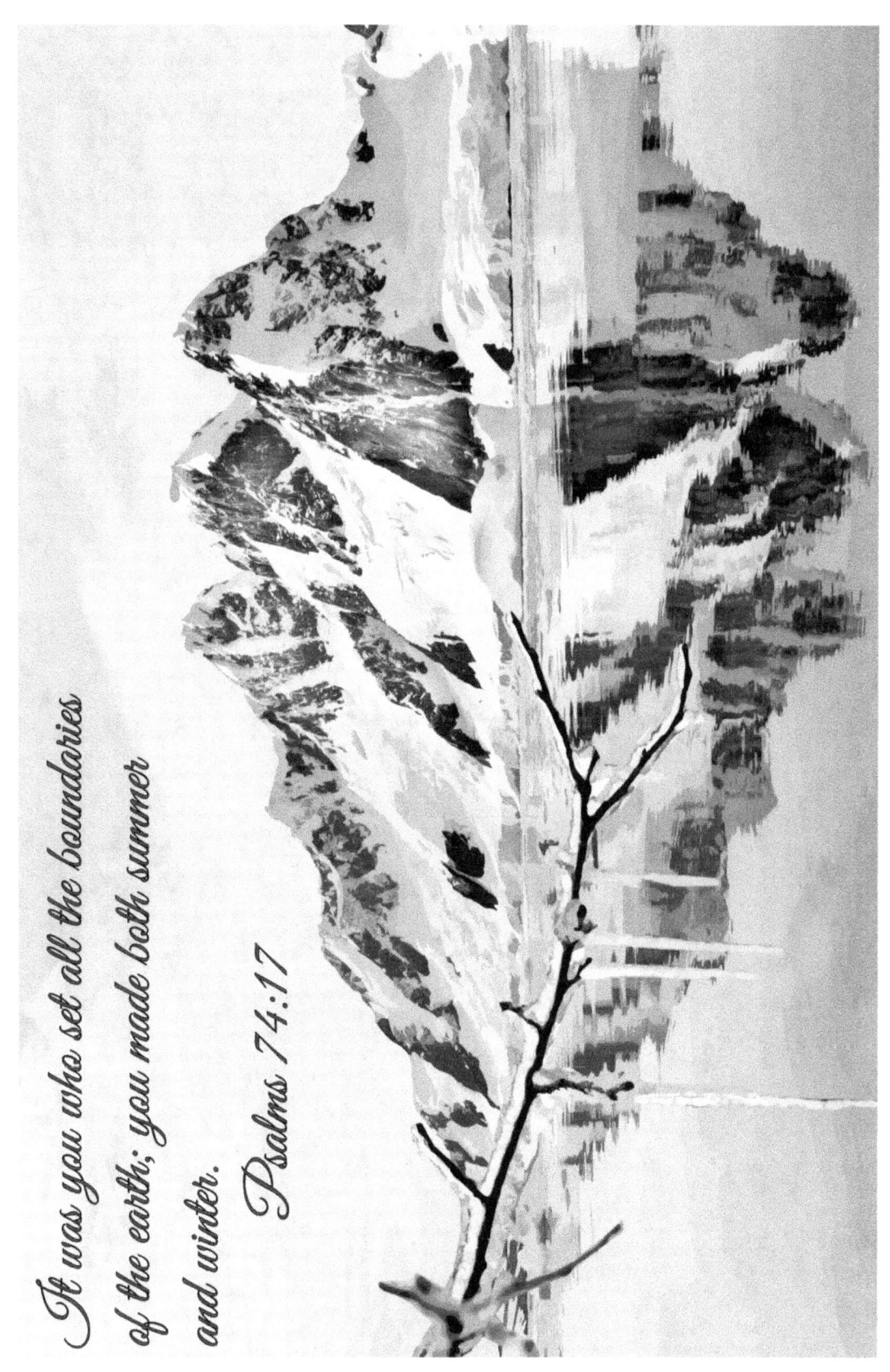

It was you who set all the boundaries of the earth; you made both summer and winter.

Psalms 74:17

Guide me in your truth and teach me, for you are God my Savior, and my hope is in you all day long. *Psalms 25:5*

He made streams come out of the rock and caused waters to flow down like rivers.
Psalms 78:16

...I lift up my eyes to the mountains, where does my help come from? *Psalms 121:1*

Let not your hearts be troubled.
Believe in God; believe also in me.
John 14:1

But blessed is the one who trusts in the Lord, whose confidence is in Him. They will be like a tree planted by the water that sends out its roots by the stream. *Jeremiah 17:8*

My soul wait thou only upon God, for my expectation is from Him. Psalms 62:5

And there shall be signs in the sun, and in the moon, and in the stars, and upon the earth distress of nations, with perplexity; the seas and the waves roaring.

Luke 21:25

Before the mountains were born or you brought forth the world,

from everlasting to everlasting you are God.

Psalms 90:2

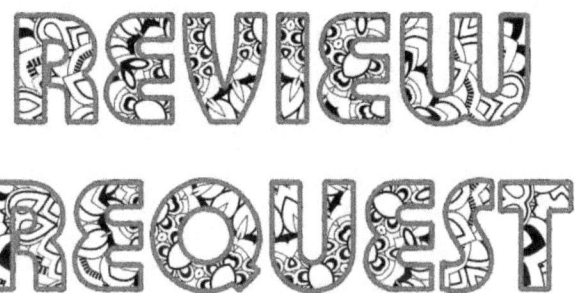

REVIEW REQUEST

If you enjoyed Yah's Majesty please consider leaving
a review at Amazon so others can enjoy it, too. Thank you!

Donna was raised in rural Indiana, and after serving in
the military, she moved to rural Kentucky. She has been
creating designs for her own pleasure for nine years,
and only recently turned to publishing them.
She lives with her husband on their nine acre farm
surrounded by woods and fields. They have a blended
family of 7 sons and 2 grandchildren, with one on the way.

Coloring is a Lifestyle.   What is yours?

ColoringLifestyles.com